#Adopted

Danielle Holder

Unless otherwise stated, scriptures are taken from the New King James Version®. Copyright © 1982 by Thomas Nelson, Inc. Used by permission. All rights reserved.

Copyright © 2021 by Danielle Holder

All rights reserved. No part of this publication may be reproduced, distributed, or transmitted in any form or by any means, including photocopying, recording, or other electronic or mechanical methods, without the prior written permission of the publisher, except in the case of brief quotations embodied in critical reviews and certain other noncommercial uses permitted by copyright law.

ISBN: 978-1-7368557-0-6

LCCN: 2021907016

Published by Danielle Holder
Printed in the United States of America
www.DanielleHolder.com

Dedication

To my mother, Dorothy Holder, until we meet again. I love you.

To my son Oshane! You have motivated me in ways no one else could.

To my siblings, especially Nicole, Debra, Joe, Michelle, Chris, and Dondrey. I love and appreciate you all.

To my foster care case workers. Thank you for having my best interest at heart!

CONTENTS

Foreword 1

Introduction 5

Chapter 1: #separation 7

Chapter 2: #BackgroundStory 12

Chapter 3: #FosterHomeNumber1 19

Chapter 4: #FosterHomeNumber2 24

Chapter 5: #Darknights 30

Chapter 6: #myadoption 36

Chapter 7: #ThingsTakeATurnForTheWorse 44

Chapter 8: #LustGrows 50

Chapter 9: #savedintheknickoftime 59

Chapter 10: #effectsoftrauma 76

Chapter 11: #ABBA 84

#BeautyForAshes 90

Acknowledgements 92

Resources 94

Foreword

As you will learn from this book, one of the greatest crises to plague the human species is the identity crises. The lack of knowledge of who we are and whose we are leaves us in an orphaned state. We do not realize that not only have we been hand selected and a huge price has been paid for our adoption BUT, as it would turn out, our adopted father is ACTUALLY our real FATHER. He wants us to spend the rest of our lives showing us how we were always His the whole time.

This is a truth that SO MANY are lacking in even though it is readily available for them. So many have been blinded by the spirit of the age and have found themselves entrenched in dark cycles of bondage, paths that lead to nowhere, and endless spirals of self-defeat and self-sabotage.

In her book "#Adopted," Danielle shares not only her personal experiences that led her to the foster care system, the dark history of abuse and neglect, the pain of what seemed to be a never-ending pattern of defeat BUT how she overcame, how she healed, how she found herself on a path to victory.

This came not only with natural adoption but truly FINDING HERSELF in the arms of her true Father and receiving the spirit of adoption which has broken her free into a life of joy and peace!

I met Danielle years ago when I was pastoring a small church in the city of Newark, DE. She was a young woman who had more questions than answers, but she had this determination in her eye to get somewhere! I'm not sure, at the time that she knew where "somewhere" was, but I knew she knew it was anywhere other than where she had been. Over the years, serving as her Pastor for a while and then later at her next church where I served on the pastoral staff, I have had the opportunity to know her and to watch her grow. I have seen her struggle, I have seen her fight, I have seen her nearly give up, and I have seen her rise to win again another day. I have seen her overwhelmed, I have seen her at peace, I have seen her unsure, and I have seen her relentlessly determined. One thing that has truly stood out to me is her ability to learn as she has been processed through life. I have seen her LIVE OUT the lessons and truly be able to pull out the life-giving principles that have brought her to her current moment.

Danielle is an overcomer. Her life is a testament to the power of God to redeem a life and bring victory out of what seemed like defeat. She has blossomed into a powerful voice for the unheard. Her personal stories and experiences will be the key that unlocks the prison of silence for SO MANY who are currently sitting in shame and locked up in their pasts.

To Danielle, I say CONGRATS; this is just the beginning. May you be all that you were created to be and may your future be SO MUCH BRIGHTER than your past. As we have talked about before, remember YOU HAVE EVERYTHING YOU NEED to accomplish ALL that He has called you to do. Everything that pertains to life and Godliness is already IN YOU. You are a daughter, and because you are a daughter, you have unlimited access to the MORE THAN ENOUGH that the Father has provided with YOU in mind.

To the reader, I say #Adopted is more than a book, more than a story: it is a weapon of war. This book serves as a battle axe in the hand of God and will crush the weighty lies that the devil has used to hold so many bound in that place of the unknown. That place where you have no idea who you are, why you are, or what in the world it was all for. My prayer as you begin to traverse through this book is that, no matter your life history, if you can identify with being in the foster care system, abused, adopted etc., OR even if none of that has been your story, my prayer is that you find yourself in this book and you allow these words to cause you to look introspectively and consider your own reality.

Are you living the life you deserve? Have you begun to walk in the understanding that you are a son or a daughter? Do you live like it? Are there areas in your life where you are still stuck in what USED TO BE or what HAPPENED TO YOU? And what would happen if you really KNEW that you KNEW that you KNEW that you were ACCEPTED in the BELOVED? You are perfectly in process, so enjoy the journey!

Pastor Carl D. Wright
Hope City House of Prayer south campus

Introduction

Trauma. That six letter word is so loaded. There are all kinds of traumas and, working as a nurse, I know those types of patients are extremely vulnerable. Trauma patients even have their own department designated to them in a hospital with trained professionals to care for them.

However, I am focusing on emotional trauma and abuse. Emotional trauma can result from a variety of sources, and yet its damaging effects usually present the same from person to person. Shame, pain, guilt, fear, anxiety, anger, among others, are some of the effects. Whether you have experienced emotional or physical trauma, the effects of that trauma can be similar.

The Merriam-Webster Dictionary defines trauma as "a disordered psychic or behavioral state resulting from severe mental or emotional stress or physical injury." The traumas I have endured include molestation, abandonment, rejection, loss, and abuse (both emotional and physical). These forms of trauma have caused severe emotional distress that led to a dulled down life. If you are a victim of trauma, I hope you read this book and it stirs something in you to seek treatment, seek God and share your story as well!

This is the first time I am sharing my full story. My wish for this book is to bring hope to those who have survived trauma, to bring awareness of the effects of abuse and trauma, and to tell you about Jesus. He is my anchor and hope, and the sole reason I am alive and well today. I pray that this book gets into the hands of those who may be dealing with abandonment/rejection, depression, and hopelessness or any other traumatic experience that appears to imprison you. Some of you have been through some serious soul-crushing, heartbreaking experiences. I fully empathize with you! May my story encourage you, enlighten you and bless you.

Some of these disclosures may be triggering or upsetting to some of you. To those who are triggered, please reach out to your support system or counselor before continuing to read. If you are upset because you are one of the individuals who did me wrong, then you should have treated me better. The devil may have used you for evil to harm me. But the Lord turned it around and used it for my good! I forgive you!

CHAPTER 1

#separation

It was a cold and unusually calm evening on January 31, 1995, when the Philadelphia Department of Human Services (DHS) came and removed my siblings and me from our home. At this time there were ten children in total that I can remember: Nicole, Joseph, Debra, Michelle, Dondrey, Chris, me, Lashonda, Dot Dot, and CJ. There was no fighting or crying, and no observable emotion from our mother that I can remember.

I did not know whether to be excited or afraid, but I can say I was very confused. It was exciting to imagine a life outside of the home that caused so much pain and stress. I endured abuse and trauma that no child should ever experience. So getting packed up and taking a ride with all my siblings was exciting.

Getting away from our abuser and going into the arms of warm strangers seemed satisfying. A handful of our things were packed in black plastic bags and hauled into the trunks of the cars that came to pick us up. "What is going on?", I curiously thought. I could not comprehend what was actually going on, and I definitely couldn't see past the moment to know what was going to happen. I had no idea my life was about to drastically change. All I knew was that my mom's boyfriend, "Clifford" (renamed for privacy purposes), would not be able to hurt us anymore. I am not able to remember if Clifford was present at the time, but I suppose he wasn't there. He was being accused of abuse, so his presence probably wouldn't have been a great idea.

That night about three to five DHS workers showed up, packed our things, and packed us into a couple of cars. I was in a car with my brother Chris, the sixth child of the bunch. His caramel yellow face was reassuring me that I would be okay, and that he would protect me. Chris was always a very protective brother. He would fight anyone he could to keep me safe. He was just eighteen months older than I was, but he behaved like a father towards me and the younger siblings. He was a lot like my brother Joseph, who was the oldest boy. Joseph was different though. He was not wild and unruly like the rest of us. He seemed wise, calm, sweet and protective. His had dark sun-kissed skin like our mother's. And his tall frame always made me feel safe.

The car my brother Chris and I rode in went to a shelter called St. Vincent's-Tacony Emergency Shelter care facility. I remember this shelter being full of children I believe between the ages of three and eight. As we were walking in, all the children were preparing for bed. On arrival, I was handed over to a black woman who didn't seem very friendly. She did not smile or comfort me. "Are you potty trained?" was all she asked me. I had no idea what potty trained meant, so I remained silent out of fear of saying the wrong thing. I refused to talk to anyone that night, and she didn't know if I was potty trained or not, so she put a diaper on me.

"What the hell is this lady doing?", I thought to myself (yes, I cussed as a child). I was so confused, and I thought, "maybe everyone gets a diaper." After finishing my intake, I was escorted to a large family room area where I saw my brother Chris and quickly ran over to where he was sitting. The other children were sitting Indian style in rows watching a movie on the television.

When it was time for bed, I was separated from my brother and put into my own bed. Most of the lights were turned out, which was something I was not used to. I was completely terrified, mainly because I experienced night terrors. I was used to sleeping with all of my sisters in a bunk bed. We had a girls' room bunk bed and a boys' room bunk bed at our home. I remember being confused and scared that night sleeping in a bed alone. Why did I have to sleep at this strange place? Why am I wearing a diaper? What in the world is going on? I was extremely anxious.

That night I didn't sleep much, and I was afraid to get up to go to the bathroom. I tried so hard to hold it in until morning, but I ended up pooping on myself. Too timid and afraid to speak up, I just lay there. The smell of poop and urine began to fill the room. One of the workers came to the room and I was taken to get changed. It was another young black lady with an unwelcoming attitude. She didn't say much but her nonverbal communication made me feel completely humiliated. She huffed and puffed and made faces; her body language said it all.

I do not have any other recollection of the time I spent at this shelter. All I remember is feeling incredibly stressed and anxious. I spent almost 3 months at this shelter. Now you are probably wondering what events lead up to this. Keep reading the next chapter will explain!

CHAPTER 2

#BackgroundStory

I want to give you a little history of my biological family. Let me take you on a chronological journey of events that led up to our family's separation. Our family had been involved with child welfare since September 1981! That's nine years before I was even born!

My biological mother had my eldest sister Nichole in 1980; she then had another daughter Diesha in 1981. Diesha was born with fetal alcohol syndrome. CPS (child protective services) became involved when she was found to have multiple injuries coinciding with abuse and neglect. Reports were made from the hospital when Diesha was found to suffer from fractures to her head, shoulder, and both legs. She also suffered from a brain hemorrhage that resulted in loss of brain function. I don't know what kind of horror this child endured as the reports I read were limited. She had diaper rash and bug bites on her body as well. The reports I read did not give the age of death, but she could not have been much older than twelve months.

Our mother was claimed to be the perpetrator of the abuse and was arrested in January 1982 and sentenced to a minimum of three years in February 1983. I do not know the amount of time she served but it could not have been very long because my next sibling was born in October 1984. I honestly don't know if she actually killed my sister or if she was covering up for someone. I believe the latter part but cannot be certain. After serving time, my mother was released and shortly after, met my father, who also had been just released from jail. I was told by family members on my biological father's side that they met coming out of jail. What are the odds ha-ha? My mother and father had five children together, Joseph, Debra, Michelle, Dondrey and me. They were a very odd and toxic couple. There was also a huge age gap between them. My father had 2 daughters before he met my mother, who were close to my mother's age! My mother had me when she was 26, while my father was 50. And I was their last child!

We lived in a two-story row home somewhere in north Philly with a creepy unfinished basement. I remember there were large holes in the wall, and filth everywhere. My mother was nowhere to be found at times. She could have been working but I do not remember if she had a job or not. She seemed withdrawn and emotionally detached. My mother had been receiving services from Services to Children in their Own Home (SCOH) since 1987, a program that helps prevent out-of-home placement of children. The goal was to "stabilize family functioning" and prevent us from having to be placed in foster care or group homes. These services began after the birth of my sister Michelle, child number four.

There had been reports to child protective services regarding all my mother's children. Countless reports were filed over the years, though many of them were unsubstantiated. Reports of neglect, no diapers or food in the house, drug abuse by my mother, lack of adult supervision – the list goes on. I am still in shock that some of the reports came back unsubstantiated because I lived it and they were true.

On various occasions, I have been told by family members – and have actually seen some reports – that my mother did cocaine and drank alcohol throughout her pregnancies with my siblings. Some of us were born with Fetal Alcohol Syndrome. I did not find any reports of me being born addicted to any drug, but I would not be surprised if she did.! Many more reports were filed, until the day my siblings and I were taken from our home. We went through so much pain during the time we spent with our biological mother, even homelessness at some point. It was a very unstable and turbulent time.

My biological mother left my dad at some point and met Clifford. He was a cruel man, who was the father of my younger siblings. His demeanor was that of a dictator and he would soon become known to me as an abuser. I will never forget what he looked like: tall, light-skinned with soft black hair. In fact, I remember him more clearly than I do my mother. I feared him, and so did most of my siblings. Except Debra, she always challenged him. He was a predator! Militant and unemotional. He would abuse my mother in front of all the children with no remorse. I remember watching him beat my mom and oldest sister in front of us. He terrorized our whole family, and my mother and oldest sister got the worst of it. He would also come down hard on my brother Dondrey. Dondrey was an ornery dark-skinned little knucklehead. I loved him so much. He taught me everything I know about fighting and expected me to always win.

Clifford would force my mother into sexual acts with him, while the youngest children, including me, watched them. He would walk into their bedroom, while we were there, and have his way with her. I can remember him being very forceful, and my mother just whimpering and looking so helpless. It soon became "normal" to me. Nothing shocked me anymore: abuse became part of my everyday life. I can remember him throwing my sister Nicole down the stairs in front of us and just watching her scream and cry. This was all happening before she was five and caused long lasting PTSD.

Many times he would lock my siblings and me in our rooms. We would be locked in for hours at end, with nothing to eat or drink and when we did eat it was mostly bread and water. He would beat us with belts and other objects on a regular basis, not just for the sake of discipline, but for us to fear him, I believe. We got so creative that we would train each other to cry and scream even if we didn't get hit, so he would stop. It worked, most of the time.

I remember one specific time I was in trouble with him and encountered his anger face to face. I had eaten a piece of bacon off of his plate when he was not looking. And he knew it was missing but didn't know who did it. He yelled and made a big deal of it and found out that I did it. He made my siblings bring me to him. I can remember trembling before him. He was playing a video game, stopped, then smacked me so hard across my back I immediately threw up. That made him furious. I was only three or four years old then!

Food was often off limits in our house or just not there. One night my older siblings devised a plan to get us all a snack. We snuck downstairs during the night in the dark and made bologna and mustard sandwiches without bread. Not long after we snuck downstairs, he woke up. I believe he was under the influence of some drug because we didn't get caught. I know the Lord was watching over us that night. I can't imagine what he would have done to us if we had been caught. He didn't even look in our rooms! He came downstairs and we all hid under the dining room table. It was just a handful of us that came down to eat. As he came downstairs, we laid on the dining chairs under the table while the tablecloth covered us up. We watched his feet walking to the kitchen and back. My heart was beating so fast; all I could think about was getting caught and beaten up. Not a peep came out of any of us!

Everyone in the house experienced sorrow and pain. The atmosphere of our home was so dark and heavy. Fear and intimidation were a common theme that hovered over our home. The house was dimly lit and messy all the time. The carpet was worn down and gritty. The kitchen was unthinkable. There were always maggots everywhere even under the couch at times. I think my siblings used to do that to prank us. I developed a maggot phobia so bad I wouldn't eat anything that resembled them, especially rice, or rice crispy treats, for years. To my detriment, these small creatures were triggers that carried into adulthood.

CHAPTER 3

#FosterHomeNumber1

In April 1995 I was placed in my first foster home. It was a scary, dark, and traumatizing time for me. I remember my first foster mom being mean and harsh with me. She wasn't very understanding and had no idea how to handle a traumatized child. I'll call her Sheila for privacy reasons. I don't actually remember her name and I hope that's not her real name! Anyways, Sheila was a heavy handed and aggressive black woman in or around her 40's or early 50's, or at least that is how she looked. Cruelty and nastiness are not good for the skin! She came off as cold and uncaring. She treated the other children she had more gently than me. I used to believe she was a witch or the black version of the ugly stepmother in Cinderella ha-ha. I had a very robust imagination.

I remember crying almost every day while I was with her. I was frequently put on punishment and sent to be in a dark room after getting beatings. There were dark colored curtains that blocked the sunlight from the windows, so it was always dark in the girl's room. I was alone a lot and did not understand why I was treated so badly. I was already suffering from rejection, and this did not help make it any better. It seemed like she beat me for anything, and I felt like I never knew why. I felt worse off being there and longed to be back home with Clifford and my mom. I felt consumed by pain and loneliness during this time. The night terrors and tormenting dreams continued and intensified during this time. I was afraid to go to sleep most nights and would wake up tired and exhausted most days. I tried so hard to stay up and not go to sleep at night because the terrors seemed inevitable.

There was one particular day where we were walking somewhere, and I remember being so hurt and devastated. I had this favorite outfit that I loved to wear. I wanted to wear it every day! It was a denim outfit with a matching hat with yellow and white flowers on it. Sheila took it from me and gave it to one of the other little girls. "No this heffa didn't" I thought, but too afraid to say. When I think about it now, maybe I grew out of it; but the way she took it from me still hurt. You know that choked up feeling you get when you're about to cry but don't want to let it out? when it feels like you have a lump in your throat? That is how I felt that day and most of the time at this foster home. I was hurt to my core!

I walked behind everyone else that day, my thoughts going crazy, my head hanging down. Alone was an understatement. I felt abandoned, and unworthy of love. I would have accidents on myself during the day and night and felt like I had no control over it. I never had an issue with wetting myself until then.

Sheila quickly lost her patience with me. I remember one summer day I had an accident, which wasn't out of the norm, and it really pissed Sheila off. I mean PISSED! She took me to the bathroom to give me a bath. She was so rough with me, it felt like she nearly scrubbed my skin off. She washed me so thoroughly; yet I had never felt so dirty, like I was filthy and unclean, and no amount of soap could cleanse me. She scrubbed in between my legs so hard, my private part hurt for a few hours. She handled me so carelessly. That day I cried myself to sleep.

You are probably wondering why I didn't tell someone. Up until this point I'd experienced so much trauma, pain, and change that I didn't know what was right or wrong. I didn't know what peace and love really meant, or what it felt like to be cared for lovingly. I was in constant angst and fear. Always on my guard, angry and anxious, I didn't know how to speak up for myself. I was afraid and thought that if I spoke up Sheila would retaliate. It wasn't much different from the abusive home I was taken from. I had never experienced an adult sticking up for me, so I had no faith that if I spoke up, I would be rescued.

My family and I continued to have visitations because the goal was to go back home once things stabilized. I longed for our visits and was excited to get to see them all again, even my mother. My favorite times were when I would get piggyback rides from my brother Joe. They made me so happy! My sister Debra would lecture me on how to act, what to say, and to not trust anyone! I was not allowed to tell anyone what really went on in our home because, if I did, we would never see each other again. At least that's what Debra told me.

Debra was our little mother; she kept everyone together. She looked most like our mom and was strong-willed and persistent. My sister Michele was sweet and quiet. I remember her being the most hopeful and kind. We all would play together, laugh, and love on each other. Our time together seemed to pass so quickly and, before I knew it, we would be separated again. I'd have angry fits when it was time to part from my siblings.

I could never understand why it was taking so long for us to live together again. My mother would tell us all the time that we would be together again. She and Clifford would promise to get me my own bed and bring us all home. I dreamt of that day for an awfully long time. I'd picture all of us together in our family room, eating cereal, sitting on the couch and being silly. That day never came. Visitations continued but I didn't get to see my sister Nichole much after the separation.

Nichole was so gentle and sweet. She was light-skinned with long beautiful hair. She was always daydreaming and seemed sad most of the time. One of my earliest memories of her was one I will never forget. She and I sat in the family room with dim lighting. She held me in her arms and lap on the couch. Tears rolled down her face, but no sound came out. I was so perplexed. I never knew crying could be so quiet, yet so loud. Little did I know that I would come to know that phenomenon all too well. The feeling of deep emotional and inescapable pain!

CHAPTER 4

#FosterHomeNumber2

In November 1995 I was moved to my second foster home. It was clean, bright, and homey. I remember it smelled like vanilla and lavender with a slight hint of moth balls. The living room had hardwood flooring with plastic still covering the cream colored couch set and pillows to match. The kitchen looked like a small Italian restaurant with a red colored tabletop island and red leather bar stools. The dining room was decorated beautifully with a modern Asian themed décor. Red, gold, and dark walnut were the colors. It was my favorite place in the house because of the large stereo. I would dance and lip sync to Mariah Carey and Brandy songs all day long in that room.

There were other foster children around the same age as me in the home. I finally felt like I could breathe here and let down my guard. My new foster mom had the same name as my birth mother, Dorothy, and the same last name as me, Rogers! My little five year old mind could not grasp the concept that two people could have the same name. "Well she has the same name as my mom, so she must be my mom too." I thought. She greeted me with the sweetest, warmest, heartfelt smile I'd seen in a while. She reminded me of my social worker that I had at the time. They were both so kind and accepting.

I arrived at her house with one black plastic trash bag, full of urine-stained clothes and shoes. Sheila didn't bother to wash them; she just threw them in the bag. This was thrift store winter clothing and underwear that she cut up to make into spring and summer clothing when it got warm. My mom later told me the story of how Sheila bragged about this. I watched as my new foster mom opened the bags and jerked her head back and scrunched her face up in disgust. "This smells like piss, oh no, I can't keep this!" She said. She threw all my clothes away and gave me a whole new wardrobe. She dressed me like a doll! Dresses and skirts galore!

I had breakfast, lunch, and dinner every day. She did her best to keep up with my hair, which was not her strong point though she kept it clean and combed and would take me to the hair salons for special occasions. I had never experienced such consistent loving care like this before. And even though things were wonderful, I still had this empty void on the inside that none of the gifts, fine treatment, or food could fill. Since my new foster, soon-to-be-adoptive mother was so good to me, I never had the heart to tell her that I really just wanted to go home and be with my real family.

She would quiz me on my brothers' and sisters' names, so I wouldn't forget them. She was an amazingly sweet, kind, and generous woman. Standing at only 4"11', She had the heart of a thirty foot giant. She treated me like her own child and opened her home and heart to me. She could sing like a canary! What a blessing she was! Tiny and powerful.

Let me not forget about my pop, a tall, dark-skinned, gray-haired smooth talking New Yorker! Pop could fix anything. Gifted with being a carpenter of great skill, he could build a house from scratch apart from the electrical system using a blueprint he drew himself! I haven't met anyone yet that could match his skill and expertise! Our relationship was not the great, but I honor him because he was always physically there.

Let me tell you a little more about my new foster mom. She had three older birth daughters and four grandsons. Her daughters were adults, and her grandsons were preteens and teenagers. She was a nursing assistant alongside her best friend and cousin who we all called Aunt Cynthia. These two were inseparable; they were like white on rice. My mom was a clean FREAK! I never understood how she could keep her home looking like a picture straight out of a magazine with kids in it all day long. She was my picture of a wonder woman. And how she loved each foster child is inspiring!

My foster mom did a fantastic job of taking care of me. The other children called her mommy Dot, but I called her mom because she was a mother. She shared her story with me when I was an adult. She said when she was younger, all she wanted to do when she grew up was to be a mother. That's all she wanted, and she did it well!

The other foster kids began going home to their families one by one. I secretly envied them. There was only me and another little girl who remained. We lived at 77th and Ogontz Ave in West Oak Lane in Philadelphia, PA. This became my new childhood home. Visitations with my birth mom and siblings began to slow down and become very inconsistent until they stopped completely upon my adoption. I will discuss more about my adoption later. I had started outpatient therapy in April 1995 at age four and continued when I came to this foster home. My treatment plan included family therapy, community based therapy, play therapy, and role playing. This also ceased when I was adopted.

During my early days at this foster home my foster mom threw me the biggest birthday party I ever had. It was the only birthday party I ever remember having. I was turning six and was excited and confused at the same time. I couldn't remember turning five! In my mind I was turning five because I didn't have a party for my fifth birthday. I didn't even realize I had turned five (I turned five when I was with that awful lady Sheila). I argued with my foster mom until she finally gave up and told me I was turning five and six, ha-ha.

I remember this day like it was yesterday. It was either June or July of 1996- DJ cool's song "Let me clear my throat" blasted through the speakers. I daydreamed of my sisters dancing with me and having a good time. I wanted to be more present and involved at the party, but I was so distracted by my thoughts of one day being home with my real family. It seemed surreal to me like I was going to wake up one day and be back with my family. At the same time, I had a great time that day. And baby, let me tell you, I ate so much watermelon and blue crabs, I nearly forgot all my troubles! You could not find a 6 year old on the east coast who could crack and eat blue crabs like me haha.

My foster mom celebrated me, mothered me, disciplined me, and loved me. And although the situation in my birth home was far from ideal, I still longed to be back with my mother and siblings. I would cry myself to sleep for years until I just suppressed the feelings in an attempt to forget. I would wait until everyone was asleep and just cry, silently. Remembering my sister Nicole who I watched cry without making a sound, and thinking, "Wow, this is the pain she felt!"

CHAPTER 5

#Darknights

I began to blossom at my new foster home! I started school, made friends, and gained some healthy weight! I was dressed in the best clothes The Children's Place could provide. I felt safe and cared for. But unbeknownst to me, I was being preyed on and groomed (the slow meticulous process a predator uses to get children to trust them).

One day, one of my favorite neighbors lured me into his basement. This was a man that everyone knew and loved. He was a scruffy old gray haired man who I assume was retired. He sat on his porch all day and watched everything! He had a basement full of toys! Mountains of them. He had so many toys piled up that it was impossible to walk around, except in a cleared pathway that lead from the basement door to the exit. He was careful to build rapport with me. I trusted him. He was nice and charismatic. The look in his eyes seemed familiar, but I did not know why. He looked at me as if he saw ME, and I was the only little girl in the world. He would tell me that I was his girlfriend, and that made me feel special.

One afternoon he told me to meet him in the basement and he would give me a toy. Running around the block to get to the back of his home brought me so much excitement. I rarely got new toys, so this was a treat. He'd let me play with the toys before but never let me have one! I ran around to the back of his home and he let me into the basement. It was pitch black inside. I stepped in and that was the beginning of a nightmare. He picked me up and sat me on top of something similar to a large filing cabinet. As I sat there, face to face with him, this eerie feeling came over me. Then he kissed me on my mouth and paused – like he was giving me a moment to respond. I didn't say a word. I did not have the language to even begin to explain what was happening. He began molesting me and making me do things to him I won't write about here. This went on for years. I was too afraid to say anything and immediately felt shameful.

I began to think that this was normal. I had seen my birth mother and older sister being sexually violated, so why would it be any different for me? I would have nightmares for years that if I told anyone my new family would die. I believed the lie that what I had to say didn't matter and my voice wouldn't be heard. So I never said a word. And I believed I was making a sacrifice to keep my family safe. He would give me toys before I left "our" spot to keep me quiet. One day he gave me a red Gideon's King James bible instead of a toy. The irony, my abuser giving me a bible! Nonetheless, I kept it in my room with me until I was seventeen.

He would give me alcohol to drink and act as if I was his girlfriend. He taught me how to make wine from grapes and would make me drink it when it was complete. It wasn't until my mom bought me a VHS tape called Get Street Smart: A kids guide to stranger dangers, that I realized I was being violated. I felt so guilty knowing I allowed someone to touch me. I was even more frightened to tell anyone and continued to keep this a secret. I felt like it was my fault, and that people would be mad at me. I tried avoiding my abuser as much as possible after that. He tried everything he could to get close to me as I tried distancing myself.

He tried everything he could, even persuading my foster mom to allow him to give me piano lessons. I remember being in my room at the piano I begged for and finally got for Christmas, and him walking in. I believe I was ten at the time.

I was terrified. He told me my mom let him up so that he could teach me to play the piano. He taught me a few times and tried touching me when my mom wasn't looking. I felt so trapped and didn't know how to get out of this situation. I thought, "If I give up piano he will stop coming." So I stopped showing interest in the piano after that and he stopped coming.

During the ages of five to eleven, I became a very sexualized child. I would find myself looking for opportunities to act out sexual acts that my abuser did to me and those that I saw happen to my birth mom. I did these while playing with barbies, teddy bears, even other children. And sometimes I didn't have to even look for these opportunities. They would come to me. Little boys on my block would touch me and do things to me without my permission. Kids at my elementary school would play games like, catch a girl freak a girl. I even had a young lady assault me in first grade in the girls' bathroom. She came in after me, threw me against the wall, shoved her fingers in my vagina, and ran out.

After that day I was filled with so much anger. I promised myself that I wouldn't let anyone ever overpower me again. Even from the mere age of six years old, I was full of rage. I would pick fights with kids for no reason. I was a bully! I was disobedient and reckless in the classroom. I got up and walked out as I pleased without asking anyone's permission. It was so bad that my second grade teacher wanted to press charges and call the police on me after I assaulted her for trying to stop me. I don't recall all the details, but something triggered me, and I picked up a desk and threw it at her and tried to pull her hair. I punched, kicked, and scratched her arms up. She was a slim, pale, strawberry blonde haired young woman.

I was so disruptive in school that I required a wrap-around facilitator. A wraparound facilitator provides case management kind of services to children with serious emotional issues. My wraparound would come to my school and help keep an eye on me. It didn't help, I would get sent home and they'd take me to get McDonalds or something. It got to the point, that when my wraparound was not there, I would have to sit in the front with my teacher and hold her hand during class. It never worked long enough because I would just pull away and run out the class when I wanted to. I got in fights almost every day and was sent home. The trauma I went through up to this point was so overwhelming I did not know how to process it. It showed through my volatile behavior and reactions to triggers.

Fighting was an outlet for me. Even though I was going through counseling and interventions, nothing seemed to work.

I missed lots of school time and failed every single subject. I somehow was promoted to the next grade every year. When they would test me, it would show that I was either on or above average. I would read the dictionary for fun and do schoolwork when I felt like it. I would turn in work every so often and my teachers would be shocked that it was actually correct. I continued this behavior until 3rd grade, the year I got a black teacher named Mrs. Johnson. Mrs. Johnson did not play! She pulled me aside one day after class and set me straight. I cannot remember what she said word for word, but she told me that she was not the one, and that she was not scared of me. She told me I was smart, and she wanted to see me do well in school. I did not TRY Mrs. Johnson!

CHAPTER 6

#myadoption

The day I got adopted was a sad for me. I should have been happy and grateful that my foster parents wanted me. But, on the other hand, I was also very hopeful that I would eventually go back to my biological family. The other foster children that my foster mom kept, had gone back to be with their families and I wanted the same for me. I secretly hoped and wished I could go back to my mom and thought things would be better. As the years passed, even after my adoption, I was still hopeful.

I was with my foster family from the age of five to seven before I was legally freed by the department of human services for adoption. By then my birth mother and birth father had lost their parental rights, and my birth family visitations fizzled away. I had no idea at the time that my parents had relinquished their parental rights. Just before my eighth birthday, both my biological mother and father attended the termination hearing, and both declined to participate in the closure process for me.

One day, my foster mom asked me if I wanted to be adopted. I said "Sure," but I wondered why she would ask me that. I didn't really know what it meant, and she didn't really know how to explain it to me. I thought it meant I could stay with her a little longer. I just knew I was supposed to go home and be with my birth family as my birth mom had promised a long time ago. And I believed her.

Early 1997 was the last time I saw my birth mother (I was six then). She never said goodbye or anything. It was abrupt and traumatizing. Yet I internalized it all. The day I was adopted, March 12, 1998, my middle and last name were changed. I had this sense that I was losing a part of myself and I didn't know how to deal with it. I was happy in a way, yet so sad. I had always thought I was eight years old when I got adopted but, after reading my adoption paper as an adult age twenty-five, I discovered I was actually seven. They were filled with so much information it was a lot to take in.

The document both confirmed and revealed a lot. First, I was not "taken" from my birth mother. She had signed all her children over to be temporarily committed to the department of human services of Philadelphia. It also confirmed the abuse and neglectful treatment I remembered. It had been so many years since being with my birth family I thought that maybe the things I had experienced were only dreams. The abuse, neglect, and trauma were all documented. My early counseling sessions were similarly documented, along with every psychological assessment. It showed that I was diagnosed with an adjustment disorder, anxiety, depression, PTSD, ADHD, and a learning disorder.

I often wonder, where I would be right now if I had not been adopted. What would my future look like? Who would I be right now? I think it's safe to say that the trajectory of my life has changed dramatically because of my adoption. And, although things were not perfect, it was a whole lot better than the situation I was born into, and the challenges I would have faced.

Adoption is such a powerful process. It is not a new and certainly not a manmade idea. In fact, adoption is mentioned many times in the bible. Some examples are Moses, Esther, and even Jesus! Pharaoh's daughter adopted Moses. Esther was adopted by her uncle Mordecai. And Jesus, sweet baby Jesus, was adopted by Joseph, Mary's husband.

In every single story, adoption benefited the adopted child greatly. Moses was saved from death and raised by Pharaoh's daughter as her own son. He was able to live a privileged life and had access to education and so much more. God used him mightily! Esther was raised and taught by Mordecai to be well mannered and know the things of God. She grew up to be an incredibly beautiful woman, inside and out. And as Queen of Persia, she was instrumental in saving the whole Jewish nation from annihilation. Imagine if neither one was adopted? Their lives would be so different. Moses would probably be dead. And Esther would probably be poor and homeless.

But there is an adoption that is greater than any human adoption that could ever take place, a legal action that has already been instituted for all of humanity! If you are not familiar with the bible, then let me explain very simply. God has made provision to adopt us (yes you and me) as His children! And this was not a choice he made because he saw that we were on earth messing up our lives. God planned our adoption even while we were considered His enemies. God had compassion on us, not because we were innocent adorable little orphans. But God had decided BEFORE the foundation of the earth that Jesus would die for our sins. Through His death and resurrection, he would adopt us. For those who BELIEVE, WE have the RIGHT to become sons and daughters of God.

Because of sin (that entered humanity by the sin of one man, Adam), Jesus was sent to the cross for US. To bear ALL of humanity's sin and to reconcile us to God. That's not all he did on the cross but that is not the point of my book. Jesus paid the debt that sin brings so that we can be in right standing with God. How many of you reading this would die for your enemy? How about billions of them? I'm sure not many, if any at all, would line up for this task. God made a way for our adoption while we were still His enemy. Not because we deserved it, but because of His great love and grace. The work Jesus did on the cross is priceless: to suffer a gruesome death so that we could be called sons and daughters. To pay the price, and take our penalty, and wipe our debt clean.

Now if you are not excited about that, then this next point should get you happy. Let's discuss some of the legal actions that adoption brings. Now that you understand adoption, you know that you become a son or daughter and are brought into a family. Legally, with adoption, the adopted son or daughter now has the same rights as birth children! That means WE are brought into God's family and now share the same rights as

Jesus. Eternal life and fellowship with the father! We have an inheritance! We have access!

Imagine a King sitting on his throne. No one is allowed to just waltz into his throne room, which was an old well-known rule back in the old days. If you went into the kings' throne room without being summoned or accepted, you might just get your head chopped off. Imagine this King is so gracious and loving, that he decides to adopt a bunch of unruly rebellious children and call them his sons and daughters. He gives them the same rights as his natural children. Those unfortunate children now become children of the highest power in the land and receive an inheritance. They eat and dine with the King. They are dressed in fine clothing and given everything they need. That's amazing right? But it's not until the children believe and come into the king's dwelling place, that they get to receive and experience those benefits.

So basically, there is an invitation, they believe and accept the invitation, and become the king's children. You may be thinking that is an awfully nice and kind king. But God is so much more! As I stated before, God predestined this transaction! This wasn't a plan B. God is good and has always been good. Jesus was the ONLY one who could take our place on the cross because he is sinless, pure, and perfect. He purposed for it to happen this way, and because of that, we do not have to pay the price of sin. DEATH (separation from God). We have access to God and eternal fellowship with him. We were not created to live a life without GOD! You can read all about that in the first chapters of the book of Genesis.

You also have access to the gift! It's called Salvation! There are numerous benefits to being a child of God. Our lives are completely changed, and we are given a very robust inheritance. Much larger than any trust fund, or life insurance policy that we could receive on earth. I promise you it's an inheritance you won't want to miss out on. And might I repeat, it's a gift! You can't earn this thang! Once I received this revelation, it was life-changing. I didn't get this revelation until I was twenty-eight years old. By this time both my adoptive parents had passed away in 2018. And I was left feeling like an orphan again!

Scriptures to reinforce your understanding and the concept of your identity and the spirit of adoption:

Read Colossians chapter 1 verse 19-23
Ephesians chapter 1 verse 4-14 (the whole book is dope, read it)

Danielle Holder

Galatians chapter 4 verse 5

Romans chapter 8 verse 12-17

Hebrews chapter 2 verse 10-18

CHAPTER 7

#ThingsTakeATurnForTheWorse

Shortly after my adoption, my adoptive mom was diagnosed with breast cancer. She became very ill and almost did not survive treatment. It was gloomy and unusually quiet around the house during this time. This was hard on me because I thought things were getting better. I was afraid I would lose everything, again. Her health eventually got better, but she was left with a weak heart. I began to see what sickness and infirmity could do to a person. As her health slowly deteriorated, her personality began to change. She wasn't as outgoing and exciting as I once knew. At times she would seem bitter and angry, and at other times she was her old loving, self.

When I was eleven, we moved to the state of Delaware. What a relief for me to be far away from my molester! I felt as if I were escaping and would never have to deal with those feelings again. I had hidden that pain deep inside and vowed to never speak about it. During this time, however, my relationship with my adoptive mother plummeted. She became overly condemning and strict, and I in turn became rebellious and calloused.

My relationship with my adoptive father had never been great. He was just there but not really involved. He really bonded with my younger adopted sister, and that hurt so much. It seemed he took her under his wing and kind of forgot about me. I felt so invisible. In a sense I was saved from his influence, let's just say he wasn't the most upright guy. I'd probably be a con artist at large if I were raised by him. So, although it did hurt to be rejected by a significant male figure in my life, I thank the Lord he rejected me, because it was really for my protection.

My adoptive parents, mainly my adoptive father would often use my past against me. He would say stuff like, "Your mother was a drug addict and didn't want you," or "You're lucky to be here," or "I'll give you back up for adoption." He would call me all sorts of names and look at me with disgust. This usually happened when he came home from the racetrack and when he lost the money he gambled. Sometimes, however, he could seem so nice especially in front of strangers, neighbors, and friends.

He fought a lot with my mom as well. Most of the fighting between him and my mom happened when only my younger sister and I were home. No one else in the family usually witnessed it. He would call my mom names, and it infuriated me. I couldn't believe she would let him talk to her like that. It happened mostly when she would confront him about money.

He wouldn't buy her things for Mother's Day or Valentine's Day. And when she would ask, he would say things like, "You are not my mother, so why should I get you something for Mother's Day?" I saw him as this unloving, mean, sorry excuse of a man. I hated him for so long and wanted to have nothing to do with him. I would tell my mom that I wished he would die, so we could enjoy our lives. I'm ashamed to admit this, but I would fantasize about him dying.

Some days he was happy and tolerable. Whenever he would make money from gambling or playing the horses at the racetrack he would be in a good mood. I always knew the wining days because I would wake up to him cooking breakfast. He'd cook his famous cream of wheat! Then he'd give my mom some money (probably the money he took out of the bank account). He made the best cream of wheat I'd ever tasted, so I always hoped he'd win. When he would hit big, he would promise to give me some of his winnings. He never gave me what he promised, and I stopped expecting him to.

I also felt as if my adoptive mother was unconsciously turning other family members against me through gossip and lies. She had a habit of telling one-sided stories. Her biological daughters had never been close or very sisterly towards me. I assumed the reason being the things my mother was telling them; they seemed to really disapprove and have a negative outlook of me. I would overhear her tell them that I was lazy, I wouldn't help her with my sisters' hair, or do chores. When in actuality, I was just depressed and never wanted to be around them because of the scornful treatment. The more I pulled away, the worse the contentions got. I joined clubs and sports while in high school to limit the amount of time I spent at home. There was one sister in particular who I didn't care for too much. One time she told me she would stab me and make it look like a suicide.

My nephews, who were 5-6 years older than I was, were rough with me as well and one, in particular, was really mean and would call me names. The way he would look at me would make me feel unwelcome. I also felt that my adopted grandmother, who was living with us at the time, hated me. My adopted little sister was also very cunning. She would steal large amounts of money from me and my mom.

With all this going on together with the erratic behavior of my adoptive mother, it was pure emotional chaos in the house. I felt the pain of rejection sinking its claws into me and subjecting me to anger, bitterness, and resentment. It seemed to me like I was the black sheep of the family. It was like I didn't have a voice. No one asked me what really happened, or how I felt. I had no outlet to safely express my feelings or get help and relief from the severe depression I was experiencing.

As I grew up, I hated myself and wanted to die. I often hoped that one day I would not wake up. Most of the time I was sad and depressed due to the mental battles I struggled with. The feelings of rejection were very strong. I was reminded many times by my adoptive father and adoptive maternal grandmother that my biological mother didn't want me. They would taunt me at times, saying that they would never have adopted me, and they threatened to give me back. Now, of course, I wasn't the most well-behaved of children, but that did not warrant such cruel treatment.

I found myself wishing I were back with my biological mother again. I felt as if I were a slave trying to pay a debt to this adoptive family that I could never repay, like I owed them my life. Don't get me wrong. I am grateful to have been chosen to be adopted into a family. But I was not accepted by the whole family and that hurt more than I could bear. I felt trapped by what the family spoke of me. I felt I was always being attacked. Someone would say something about me, and before investigating it, it became the truth. I was left feeling unworthy, unimportant, and so I remained quiet and secluded.

I threw myself into the only outlet that seemed to give me pleasure: porn.

CHAPTER 8

#LustGrows

From what I have previously described, you can see I had been exposed to sexual activity at a very young age. As I was always curious, I would find myself in situations, performing acts with my teddy bears and other children. I also stumbled upon my nephew's porn tape at the age of eleven. I had my own room and television with a connected VCR. Some of y'all probably don't even know what that is: just, google it! The porn tape was so enticing to me. I watched it and was immediately hooked. I would sneak and watch it multiple times a day. So there I was addicted to porn at eleven years old! It was pleasurable to indulge in this secret addiction. For a moment I forgot about the emotional pain and felt satisfied. Ten minutes of satisfaction a day was enough, but I soon found myself emptier than before. My lust grew. I wanted more. I needed more.

I started a relationship with a girl I introduced the tape to, and we would act out what we saw. My girl fascination faded quickly. I started becoming interested in men. This addiction continued for years. I even found myself at times wanting my molester. Crazy, right? I was completely overtaken by this perversion. It became my identity. It became my god in a sense; what I loved most. It felt like it was my lifeline.

With all the family dynamics going on, money was getting tight. This caused a lot of stress and fights between my adoptive parents. So, by the time I was fourteen, I was hanging out way past midnight and going to teen clubs. I wanted to have fun, to laugh, and be normal and forget my troubles. During this time, I had an increase in the amount of nightmares, and what people commonly call "sleep paralysis". It a demonic attack, but that's not what this book is about. During those encounters, I would always see demons. They would sometimes take on the form of family members and make it seem like they were going to kill me. I once saw a spirit enter my room disguised as my sister that pulled out a knife; then right before stabbing me, it turned into a vicious dog. And just before it bit me, I woke up out of the sleep exhausted and barely able to move. My arms, hands, and legs would feel like jello. This became a common event for me every night.

I would have nightmares of snakes entangling me, vicious dogs attacking me, and even falling sensations. In particular, there was this recurrent dream. I would be walking on a road in the middle of nowhere. No scenery, nothing. Just a black path like a bicycle path. The path would start to tangle me up and I would try to fight it. The more I fought it, the more entangled I got, until I was exhausted and gave up fighting. Then the path would start to smooth out and I could walk again. As always, I'd suddenly wake up full of fear and exhausted.

I would also experience physical things, too. For years I would feel something hitting me in the mouth in a way a parent smacks a child's mouth to keep them from saying bad things. It would always happen right before I was closing my eyes to sleep. I felt like I was losing my mind. How was I going to explain that to anyone? I was in so much darkness, I could feel it. It seemed so tangible. I knew when an evil demonic presence was near. I could feel it and smell it.

By the time I was fifteen, I was going to parties on a regular basis, like every Friday and Saturday. We would do this dance called grinding, which was basically girls and boys dry humping with their clothes on. It was at one of these parties that I met this guy, my first real boyfriend. We danced and exchanged numbers. We talked for a few weeks and began to meet up on the weekends. He seemed nice; he was older, so that was a plus for me! He had a car and a job! I was sold. He told me he was eighteen, but he was actually nineteen. For years I believed he was a year younger than he actually was. I should have known then that this relationship was built on lies and it would end disastrously. But I ignored the red flags.

Life at home was still miserable. Since my mom and I had a bad relationship, she stopped caring for me the way she used to. She stopped buying me necessities that I depended on her to buy, even school supplies. I tried finding a job, but I had a hard time because of my age and lack of experience. Now my mom was not just some cruel person and I wasn't an angel. I had a very slick mouth, and an "I don't really care attitude." She tried to teach me a lesson, and I tried to teach it right back. She played hardball and I'd stand my ground. I was adamant about finding my own way. So I continued to see this guy, even though I wasn't really interested in him. I even had another boyfriend at my high school at the same time.

I thought it was perfect timing for this new guy; he had money and a car. He would give me money, take me out, buy me gifts, and take me wherever I wanted to go. It wasn't long before he wanted something from me in return. Just a month or so passed, and he made his move. I felt a bit pressured to lose my virginity, because all my other friends had been having sex, and I was the last one. He also kept asking me to do it. I finally gave in, although I felt so ashamed and worthless afterward. It was like I lost a prized possession.

On the other hand, I really enjoyed it. I couldn't believe what I had been missing out on. I would do it as often as I could. I began to drink heavily and partying every weekend. I would drink Smirnoff vodka, straight – no chaser and no mix – and indulging in this pleasurable sin as often as I could. But I was never satisfied. It was as if I were chasing this high that I could never catch. It was never enough.

A year later, I ended up pregnant! Scared and ashamed, I went to Planned Parenthood to take a test and get information about abortions. I couldn't believe I sixteen and pregnant! I couldn't tell my mom; I didn't want to disappoint her, so I kept it a secret. I also didn't want to prove my family members right. They would tell me at the age 13 that I'd get pregnant before I was 18; before I was even sexually active! I was convinced by friends that I was carrying a fetus, and that it was not a baby yet, so I didn't feel bad about trying to kill it. I tried everything

I could to have a miscarriage; I even made my younger sister step on my belly. That didn't work, so I arranged to have an abortion. My boyfriend was not in full agreement, but he didn't stop me either. In fact, he drove me to the facility and gave me half of the money.

I can remember that day so clearly. It was in March 2007, and one of the most painful procedures I'd ever experienced. I didn't have enough money to get a general anesthetic, so I went through it with no pain reliever. It was the most cold, heartless, and painful experiences I have ever gone through. I could feel everything, the shoving, the cutting, the vacuuming. I remember distinctly having this feeling of empty hollowness in my stomach like something vital was taken from me. I began to cry and feel remorseful.

I started wondering if I had made the right decision. It really messed me up. After the procedure, they sat me in the recovery room with other women who had just done their procedures, too. There was a mix of emotions. Some looked relieved and unbothered, some were sleeping, and some looked like this may have been their third or fourth round. Some women were even having conversations about how many children they aborted.

I can remember before the appointment, the clinic briefed me on what to expect. They told me there would be protestors shouting and yelling at me and they reassured me that they would keep me safe. It made me feel a little bit more secure in getting an abortion, like they were helping. They told me that the people I needed to be careful around were the "dangerous and heartless" protestors.

A few months after the abortion, my relationship with my boyfriend started to get rocky. We started arguing and fighting physically. He would push or shove me, and occasionally smack me in my face. I didn't think anything of it because I was fighting him back. I started to drink more heavily, which he would buy; I couldn't figure out how he purchased it at just twenty years old. I figured his older brother bought it for him. I didn't figure out until later that he lied about his age. If I had known that then, I would have run for my life.

By the time I was seventeen years old, and a senior in high school I was in full blown rebellion. Every weekend, I would drink my favorite brands of Brandy, Bacardi, and Vodka. I would wake up with hangovers, skip school, and party as often as I could. I'd go to Philly, use fake ID's, and get into adult clubs. It felt good because it took the emotional pain away, at least temporarily.

I had been leaving home for weeks at a time by now. My mom would call and call, and I would ignore every call. If I answered, I would give her attitude, and hang up. Sometimes I'd be gone for months. In my eyes, she was the enemy; she was the one that caused me the most pain. She was supposed to help me and love me, not push me away. I felt betrayed and I did not trust her anymore. I felt like I was just some doll she wanted to dress up, and when I became boring, she lost interest in me. I had lost... my "newness" and was not good anymore.

That was my distorted reality of the truth. The fact was my mother did her best for me: she gave it her all. I knew that she loved me. She simply had not been prepared to deal with the level of trauma I had been through. She was not properly equipped, although she had good intentions. The foster care system had failed us both.

I moved out at seventeen and was living with my boyfriend and his family. I would go to school during the week when I wanted to and party on the weekends. Somehow, I still maintained a 3.9 GPA in school and managed to graduate on time. That was the grace of God because I should have flunked from the amount of days I missed. So here I was, in this mental prison of perversion and mental illness, a slave to lust and depression, self-medicating with drugs, sex and partying. I still had dreams of becoming a nurse and supporting myself. I loved the idea of making my own money and buying my happiness. So, I did everything I could by getting good grades and applying for college.

I was offered a full scholarship at Drexel University, but I declined because I wanted to be close to my boyfriend. Stupid! Plain stupid!

CHAPTER 9

#savedintheknickoftime

New Year Day of 2008 was coming and I planned to party, get drunk and celebrate as usual. But my boyfriend was behaving very unusually: he was extremely tired and did not want to do anything. It was a Monday night when my boyfriend's cousin came over and was talking about this church he went to and how he was going to a "watch night service." I had no clue what it was but something in me wanted to go. I don't remember his exact wording, but I was sold! The way he talked about this church made me feel like I should be there. So everyone except my boyfriend went to the watch night service.

I was wearing the tightest black pencil skirt I could find and a low cut shirt with stilettos. When I first walked into the service, I could feel this inexplicable thickness in the atmosphere. It was like a blanket came over me. It felt good; I'd never felt that before. Here I was at this small Jamaican Apostolic church. Music was playing, people singing, and dancing like they were drunk: it was insane. I wanted to know why they were dancing. What were they celebrating? I felt so guilty as I walked in and took a seat by myself.

The pastor came on after what seemed like hours of singing. He preached the most convicting message I'd ever heard. It was my first time hearing the gospel so clearly, even though there was a language barrier. He put a great significance on repentance. I watched my boyfriend's older brother walk to the altar and fall to the floor speaking in a weird language. I didn't know what it was at the time, but he was speaking in tongue. Then the preacher started inviting people to the altar. I was the last person to go up, I tried to stay in my seat. But I had this feeling that would be my last chance. I felt this urgency to go up, so I did.

At the altar I received prayer and accepted Jesus into my life; the next Sunday I was baptized. I was so excited to be saved and told everyone that same week. My friends all laughed at me not believing a word. My best friend at the time laughed her head off and jokingly told me to shut up. Everybody saw me as a goofy person, and they all thought I was joking.

After my baptism, I began dreaming more detailed and vivid dreams. Before, they were just nightmares, but now there was a storyline, like I was being shown things. They even felt different. One night shortly after my baptism, I had a dream I was part of this amazing ministry. I was a part of this ministry as a helper and would follow the preacher and catch people who fell under the power of God and throw blankets over them. We were visiting a hospital full of people with all types of sicknesses. The pastor of this ministry was Caucasian. When he preached, miracles would happen. People were growing limbs back and were healed from all kinds of sickness. An uproar of praise came from the hospital, a sound I'd never heard before. Nurses and doctors were bringing patients to us. Singing and instrument playing was going on.

At one point I was given the mic to preach and tell my story, and people were falling out all over. We raised offerings and the pastor turned to me and told me to take the proceeds. I didn't want to, but he insisted. The dream was so vibrant and bright, unlike any dream I had ever had before. By the end of the dream I was standing in front of three people, a Hispanic woman, a Caucasian man, and a dark African American woman, in that order. They were looking at me in a serious way, and the

Caucasian man was holding the mic out to me telling me to share.

At that point I woke up. I normally forget my dreams within minutes. But this dream never left my mind. I thought to myself, "That will never happen, and I will never follow no 'white' man." I didn't trust Caucasian preachers because I was told their power came from the devil and they were full of crap anyway. Keep reading; I am not prejudiced, I promise!

While all of this was happening to me, I was still with my boyfriend who was not saved. I was torn between living for the Lord and living for myself. I didn't want to lose my boyfriend because I felt I needed him. I would try to convince him to get saved, too, and stop smoking and drinking. When that didn't work, I would try to avoid him to keep from fornicating. But he would pressure me into doing it and convinced me that it was like we were already married, so it was okay. I continued and believed the lie. I knew that I could get pregnant, and I didn't care: we even planned to have a baby. For some odd reason I didn't think I would get pregnant due to the abortion.

But in late October, I found out that I was pregnant. This time I knew I would keep the baby. I was both excited and embarrassed at the same time. In December that year, we were married. I felt that I was talked into getting married by the church folks. I didn't think of just leaving him and going home because I wanted what I wanted. So, as they pressured me, I pressured him by telling him I would leave. Now and then I would leave, not really wanting to, and he would come back and get me wherever I was. Red flags were flying high. He was very paranoid about who I hung out with and seemed to be overbearing. But I ignored all those warnings. I thought I had to marry him because he was my first and we were going to have a baby.

So we got married. He began to drink heavily during my pregnancy. And soon after my son's birth he began to get blatantly jealous and abusive. Our marriage took a turn for the worse, not that it was the healthiest of marriages in the first place. My husband was not faithful during any part of our relationship. The abuse escalated pretty quickly from smacks to punches and kicks. If I did not have sex with him when he wanted or how long he wanted, he would go into an angry fit. He started smoking WET, which is marijuana, dipped in embalming fluid, and he would lose his mind. He would accuse me of things I didn't do, and he would do bizarre things. "Great, I married the devil!" I would think.

I would often use the restroom in the middle of the night, and on one occasion I came back to find him sitting up in bed. I lay down to sleep and woke up to him standing over me with his fist clenched. I could literally feel an evil presence behind him and, when I looked at him, his face looked distorted and incredibly angry. He did not look like himself.

"Did you ask me to use the bathroom?"

I laughed, but inside I was panicking, thinking, "What in the world got a hold of him?" It was so bizarre.

The relationship was beginning to feel like a trap. It started off enjoyable, but it had turned scary very quickly. For years, I didn't know that rape could happen in a marriage. I thought that I didn't really have a say in deciding if we had sex or not. He would force himself on me, even if I did not agree. It was worse when he was drunk. Sometimes he would give up, and verbally abuse me instead.

One day, he pressured me into multiple rounds of intercourse until it started to hurt. I finally refused and went to attend to our son who had just woken up from a nap. He came up behind me, pushed me and then came lunging at me with his fist and punched me in the mouth. This was just one of the many altercations we had and each time it got worse. I did not think it was that bad and did not categorize it as abuse because I would fight him back, too. He would say things like, "I'm going to go find a girl who won't tell me no."

I would always think, "What did I get myself into, and how will I get out?" I felt stuck, because I had messed up with my mom, and felt that I couldn't go back. I was estranged from all friends and family.

And now I had an infant under the age of one, while still in college pursuing my nursing degree. There was no way out in my eyes. When I tried to leave, he would physically restrain me or take our son and not let me take him with me. If I did make it out the door, he would throw a large glass wine bottle from our second story apartment at me. On two separate occasions he did this and both times missed me by a hair. One time I was with a friend, and she told me if I kept going back with him, he would eventually kill me. She had witnessed him in action and warned me, "He is going to kill you if you keep going back."

I took some time to see what the bible mentioned about separation and divorce. From the very beginning God sees marriage as a covenant between a man and a woman, reflecting the covenant between God and the Body of believers who form His church (Genesis 2:24; Ephesians 5:25). God honors marriage and the marriage bed is blessed by God (Hebrews 13:4). At the same time, if the marriage is broken because of adultery, then there are grounds for divorce (Matthew 19:9). It is not stated in the Bible, but the church also recognizes that a prolonged situation of abuse, whether physical or mental, is also good reason for the victim to leave that marriage for the sake of their safety and their children's.

Finally, when my son turned seven months, I moved out and separated for the first time. I was nineteen at the time and moved in with a friend from the church. The church people tried to convince me to go back. I went back and forth a few times, leaving and coming back. I left again when I was twenty, and this time I thought I was done. I was at breaking point. I wanted to just leave and have a cordial relationship with him. But he did not agree. When I did leave, he would torment me, call me names, stalk me, and threaten me. It was like hell on earth as I moved around to different houses to try and keep him away. He was very labile, which confused me and caused me to let my guard down at times, only to have him terrorize me again. He would use our son as bait to draw me in. One time he tried to run me over with his car while picking up our son., and said he was only trying to scare me.

He would also go to my parents' house and tell them I'd left him, cheated on him, and beat him, and say that all he wanted was for me to come home. They started to turn against me and treat me as if I were the one who was the perpetrator. I never told anyone about the abuse I went through while I was there. So to them, I was the bad guy, and he was the good guy. They would say things like, "Why are you so mean to him? You really hurt him." I felt so alone.

During our separation, I resorted to my old coping mechanisms to ease the pain. I started drinking again, fornicating and became even more promiscuous. I found myself in a sexual relationship with the pastor's son, which I did for the sake of revenge. Bruh! The pastors SON!!!! I thought I was getting back at my husband for what he had done to me. But I was just falling deeper and deeper into darkness.

My husband somehow found out about my activities and completely lost it. He called my phone and left threatening messages, stalked me, and verbally abused me. I would dial the police, but hang up every time, for fear of retaliation. By the time my son was one and a half, I had moved back to my mom's house. During this time, my pop and I would argue and bump heads quite often. He would call me a whore, dumb and everything but my own name. I griped him up one good time and let's just say the fights never got that far again.

Eventually my husband found a way to lure me back into the relationship, and we moved back in with each other. I needed help with bills, so I agreed. We moved in together in March 2011, but by May things had gotten really bad. I tried to put the past behind me and be a good wife. But he was still paranoid and verbally abusive. He had begged me to come back to him and assured me that he had changed. But that was far from the truth. This time it was worse. We finally agreed to separate, and that he would leave when he was able to. I started to flirt and talk to other guys for fun.

One night I went to take a shower before work and one of the guys had called my phone. My husband had answered the phone and got into an argument with the guy, saying that I was his wife and not to call back. I started to think, "Why wasn't I your wife when you were whoring in them streets?" I got out the shower and put on some clothes. As I was getting dressed, he came to me and started pushing me and mushing my head really hard. Asking me who that guy was and why he was calling my phone. I just ignored him and kept walking away. I even left the house to get away from him. I had left my car keys in the house, so I had to go back in.

He was cussing me out and asking me who was calling my phone. As I came back in the house, he started to hit me. I tried fighting back, but this time all I could do was block his hits. He began to punch me in my stomach and arm. I covered my face so that he didn't hit me there. Then he grabbed me by the arms and slung me across the room. He just kept getting angry and attacking me with an inhuman force. Whenever he would grab me around the waist and throw me to the ground, I would punch and scratch and bite as much as I could. This time was different, my attempts to hurt him did not seem to faze him.

He took my phone at one point, bent it in half, and threw it at my head. Fortunately, the phone missed me, but put a huge dent in the wall. I then ran to the room to get a weapon, and he ran after me and caught me before I got something in my hand. He threw me to the floor and jumped on top of me and began choking me with both of his hands. I remember hoping my son was not in the room to see me die because I was sure this was it. I felt lightheaded and stopped fighting after feeling limp. I remember looking into his eyes, not recognizing him at all. His brown eyes were all black.

All I could do was call on Jesus over and over again in my head, "Help me, Jesus!" Suddenly, he just let go, got up and walked away like nothing happened. I eventually sat up confused and worn out. I thought I would surely die, and then he just walked away like he hadn't just tried to kill me.

I looked at the time and noticed I had to be at work that night in 30 minutes. I got myself together and walked to the living room. There he was sitting on the couch with our son. He looked at me and then back at the TV like everything was cool. I was furious. I told him that if he was home by the time I got off in the morning, things were going to be bad for him. I knew then that I'd had enough, and things had to change. I told God I would kill him if I came home and he was still there.

I went to work that night doing an overnight shift as a CNA. If you know anything about CNA work, you know it's physically taxing. I was sore and severely bruised. One of my friends and coworkers noticed the bruises and handprints on my neck, and gasped. She had told me about a protection from abuse and convinced me to get one. That morning after work, she and I went to the courthouse to file a Protection From Abuse order. By the time I got home, he was gone. Thank God he'd left, because I was ready to do about 12 years to life in prison.

He never stepped foot into the apartment again. Things were set up to where we met at the police station for drop offs and pickups for our son. Even after the order was in place, he would still verbally abuse me. But I would ignore him and get on with my life. I was still going to nursing school but took a small break. It took me five years instead of four.

After my graduation I fell into a deep depression and began soul searching. I didn't

know who I was, why I was living, and had no desire to live any longer. I had been depressed most of my life, and on two different occasions had attempted suicide. I was exhausted and completely at the end of myself. I remember talking to God about going back to church, but I didn't know where to go. I told God if He would show me where to go, I would go.

One night in February of 2014 I had a very disturbing dream. The dream started out as me waking up in my home. It was a dark and gloomy day. I walked outside and there was screaming, weeping, and chaos everywhere. I knew the rapture had happened. To those who are not sure what the rapture is, it's the time prophesized in the bible when Jesus comes back, and true believers are caught up with Him in the clouds (1 Corinthians 15:52). I said to myself, "Oh crap, I got left behind!" I went to look for my brother, because I knew that if I was left behind, he would definitely be left behind, too. I was walking along the street where people were looting stores, fighting, running; there were car accidents everywhere, fires and alarms going off. Just pure chaos! I never ended up finding my brother and thought, "That son of a gun got raptured after all!"

As I was walking, I saw my son's father walking towards me. We just looked at each other and shook our heads. We began walking together in silence. I looked ahead and saw a child lying on the side of the road with his back towards me. I went to look at him to see if he was okay, and he turned around: it was my son. I reeled at the sight as if my heart had dropped into my stomach. At that moment, an extremely loud sound woke me from the dream. I literally jumped out of my sleep. My heart was racing and sweat was oozing from my head. There was my son fast asleep next to me. I was so confused and amazed at how he could sleep through that noise. It sounded like a natural disaster, like the ground was struck by something large. It was like a breaking sound.

I jumped out of bed and began repenting, I was completely shaken up for a few hours. I remember begging God to at least take my son. When that didn't work, I started calling people I knew who were likely to be raptured. My train of thought was, "If these people answer, then I know the rapture didn't happen." Of course, no one answered at 2:30 in the morning. I started freaking out, but then I remembered I lived in a very unsaved neighborhood. I ran outside and looked at the sky and the ground to see if maybe something had fallen out of the sky and hit the ground. No one else was stirred like me, and I began to think I was crazy. I eventually went back to sleep, but I prayed before I did. I told God, "I'm going back to church because I can't live like this anymore."

A week or two later, I researched a few churches, and inboxed a few people about their church. But I didn't feel that any of them would be the place I needed to go. I finally saw this Facebook post on a high school friend's page about this Valentine's Day event at this church called "The Voice Ministries." I stalked the page for a few days and decided to inbox the pastor. Pastor Carl D. Wright was kind and didn't get annoyed by my series of questions. After my short "interrogation", I decided to visit the church. I couldn't believe I was going to a church with a "white" pastor. I didn't think I would fit in; I thought it would be a bunch of white folks sitting down singing hymns. Nothing wrong with singing hymns; it's just not my type of scene.

But I walked into the church and was greeted coming in and going out with a hug. And, to my surprise, my old high school friend was there. I felt a bit more at ease. I also noticed that there was a good mix of nationalities. I was a bit thrown off guard. It most definitely wasn't what I had expected. The music was popping, and the atmosphere was welcoming. The delivery of the word was spot on – exactly what I needed. Pastor Carl broke down the word clearly and precisely so I could understand it. It was the first time I felt conviction and not condemnation.

And that was the beginning of my healing process! I was reintroduced to God as my Father, as a Father who I could trust my heart with, as a Father, who liked and loved me. It was as if I was just starting to live. It was so refreshing. What I remember and treasure most about this church was that we did life together. We were a family. It was just what I needed and longed for. So much healing and growth took place in this ministry.

CHAPTER 10

#effectsoftrauma

Trauma and abuse have a negative impact on so many lives and affect every facet of your being. They come in uninvited and defile your innocence and leave a stain. They have a way of creeping into every decision you make. They affect your future. I am not an expert on the effects of trauma; I just know what happened to me and how it negatively impacted my life. It changed my entire life, forcing me to live well below my potential. My decision-making skills, choices, and social skills were greatly impaired.

The trauma experienced led me into a lifestyle of sexual perversion. I embraced it because it felt good! It ruled my life. The invisible shackles and yokes kept me engulfed in this lifestyle, even after I realized what I was doing. I was deceived and had no idea of its depravity. It presented itself as a beautiful package, but inwardly it was filled with rotten substances and maggots, sent to destroy my life, eat me alive, and keep me loyal to my own pleasures. It deprived me of the truth. I was a walking zombie, dead on the inside, and a slave to my selfish sinful desires.

When you are exposed to toxic stress as a child, it increases your risk of adverse issues and mental conditions. There is this study called the ACE score study, standing for Adverse Childhood Experience score, which is used to determine your risk of developing chronic health conditions or anti-social behaviors. For each trauma you mark yes to, your score increases, the higher the score the greater your risk. The study found connections between the ACE score and conditions such as adult alcoholism, depression, domestic violence, and chronic diseases.

I watched a TED talk by Dr. Nadine Burke Harris, that talked specifically about childhood trauma and studies that show it increases the risk of disease. The study originally done by Dr. Vince Felitti and Dr. Bob Anda at the CDC proved that ACEs have a huge impact on your future. Why? Dr. Nadine stated that "exposure to early adversity affects the developing brains and bodies of children." Brain development is so crucial in the early stages of life. Learning, decision-making, and responses to events are affected due to the early exposure to stress. She then warned, "There are real neurologic reasons why folks exposed to high doses of adversity are more likely to engage in high-risk behavior." But even those who don't engage in those risky behaviors are at risk. Our brain is like our control center, receiving and sending messages to the rest of our bodies.

Dr. Nadine then went deeper by explaining how, when children are exposed to trauma, it activates the flight or fight system in our brain. The fight or flight system is a stress response system that works by your brain sending messages to the part of your body that releases stress hormones when you are in a scary situation. You see a lion in your backyard as you are barbequing; your brain activates the flight or fight, your body responds, and you fight the lion or you run from it. I'm sure you would all run, but that is an example of your flight or fight reaction in layman's terms. So your body releases this stress hormone and you do what you need to do, fight or run.

Now repeated activation of this system is not good; it's there for you to be adaptive and useful. It's never meant to be activated every day because of your abuser or stressful situation.

Dr. Nadine goes on to say that "High doses of adversity not only affect brain structure and function, they affect the developing immune system."

So, as I watched the video I was thinking "Well dang, I was born at a disadvantage." I had a great deal of odds stacked against me. I'm talking about major setbacks. I was born into this dysfunction, and I didn't have a fighting chance. I remember reading a report that stated my mom said her pregnancy with me was troublesome. So there you have it: I was a statistic before I was even born, already labeled less fortunate and disadvantaged. And to top it all, I am an African American female, who is already in an "At risk" population. Studies say that we have some of the lowest percentages of successful marriages, education, and other achievements, along with higher percentages of mortality rates, health problems, and other negative conditions. My ACE score is a 10, which is the highest score possible.

I started to look back at decisions, thought process, and habits in the course of my life. It certainly made sense that what I had been through had shaped and molded me into the person I was. But that knowledge bought me no relief. And I asked myself again, why in spite of making up my mind to follow Jesus Christ, why was I still bound by sin? I needed deliverance. It wasn't enough to just say I followed Christ: I needed healing and I needed to be an active participant in that healing. Fear was a major issue in my heart. I felt rejected and didn't speak up when I should have. I also felt condemned, which kept me from praying, and pride kept me from seeking help.

While I wanted to be free, I believed the narrative of the devil that I wasn't worth it. I blamed circumstances for giving me the short end of the stick in life. I felt as if I were in a lower category of Christians and didn't deserve. How totally deceived I was! In the bible Jesus Himself says, "*The thief does not come except to steal, and to kill, and to destroy. I have come that they may have life, and that they may have it more abundantly*" (John 10:10). Those words "more abundantly" tell me that God didn't just save us from His righteous wrath, but came to bring us into the fullness of life. What I had believed about myself was a lie from the pit of hell. My ACE score did not have to define me. Its true trauma is damaging, but no amount of trauma is too hard for God to heal I didn't have to settle for being depressed! I didn't have to carry my shame and regret. The word says He gives us the garment of praise for the spirit of heaviness (Isaiah 61:3). I could exchange this heaviness, this depression for His garment of praise! Because I believed that I was too damaged and too messed up, I did not even expect to be completely healed. Let me tell you, that is deception. God is more than able to heal and deliver. HE is a mighty Deliverer. The word says that "*by His stripes (wounds) at Calvary we are healed*" (Isaiah 53:5). Through the severe beating He took for us, He overcame every single illness and infirmity, mental and physical.

You see, all along I had been running mostly on will power. I thought that if I could just do right, then God would help me. If I stopped "sinning," God would finally accept me and make me new. I had allowed God in – but only so far: I gave Him only a portion of my heart. The other portion was too dirty to share with Him. Because of my holding back, I didn't really allow Him to do a complete inner transformation of my mind, my will, and emotions. Your willpower is not powerful enough to do the inner work. If it were, we would not need the BLOOD of Jesus.

Richard Foster says in his book *Celebration of Discipline*, "Will power will never succeed in dealing with the deeply ingrained habits of sin." You think you are getting along fine but wait until a trigger comes and catches you off guard. What is in you will come out, and no amount of willpower can stop it. I remember leaving church and feeling so good. When I got home, my sister picked a fight with me and the next thing we were fist fighting and cussing each other out. No amount of willpower can heal you or change you from the inside. You may present to the world like you've been transformed but deep down inside you are still bleeding. Richard Foster continues about will power, "It is incapable of bringing about the necessary transformation of the inner spirit." He later concludes that "inner righteousness is a gift from God to be graciously received."

It wasn't until I completely embraced the gift and love of God, that I was able to experience the inner healing I so greatly desired. I had hidden myself for years, trying to battle the evil thoughts and desires with my willpower. That left me completely exhausted. And, let me tell you, I am one tough momma. I am not weak and I ain't a pushover. I am determined and strong. But the kingdom of God is so different. You don't attain the benefits of it in your strength or willpower. We cannot wrap our human minds around this gift because it's not a human concept. Understand that salvation is a free gift of God, and so are all His gifts. You receive them by faith.

For it is by grace you have been saved, through faith—
and this is not from yourselves, it is the gift of God—

not by works, so that no one can boast (Ephesians 2:8-9 NIV).

Gifts are meant to be received, not something you have to work for or earn. So, if inner righteousness is a gift from God, then it is by His power that I can receive His healing and transformation.

Once I had this revelation, I stopped trying so hard to clean myself up and I presented myself to God just as I was. It's God's job to do the inner changing and it's our job to trust him. He does the inner work with our participation. And participation is key! We don't just wait around doing nothing and hoping for God to do the work. We need to work with Him. My participation involved the following: showing up at church (strong faith-based church), praying (and listening), fasting, spending time with God, studying the Word and allowing the Holy Spirit to lead me. It involved positioning myself to receive from the preaching and teaching, consistently seeking Him even when I messed up. You got to show up and do the work. It's not as hard as you may think it is. When you love God, you will do what He says to do. And when you do what He says to do, you will love Him even more. It's a beautiful cycle of loving and obeying!

CHAPTER 11

#ABBA

My view of God as my Father had been completely distorted. I'd never had the opportunity to experience what a good father was like. It turned out that every male figure in my life was selfish, mean, and prideful. The father figures I had in my life were physically, verbally, and emotionally abusive. My adoptive father was a poor role model. He was disrespectful to my mother (his wife)! He would cuss my mom out and steal from her to go gamble. He was very prideful, dishonorable, and mean.

When I first came to live with them as a young child, I thought he was a nice man. He had hand painted the girl's bedroom walls a beautiful mural of birds and flowers on a lavender backdrop and an actual bird cage hung from a corner. Within three days, I saw this nice kind man turn impatient and intolerant. As I sat in my new room with my favorite teddy bear, He came in to look at his work, gloating about it while he ate popcorn. He dropped a few pieces on to the floor. When I told him, he sharply turned towards me and told me to shut up. Then he smiled and turned back and looked at his work, whistling as he walked out the room. That moment scared me, and that's just what I did. I shut up and didn't corrected him again. Until I became an unruly teenager.

As I got older, I didn't give two flips about what he thought or said And there were many more altercations between him and I. If things didn't go his way, everyone in the house felt it. He would lie and, when caught, he would get livid as if he were being wronged. Our fights began to escalate as I became a teenager. I never listened to him and became very disrespectful towards him. I would cuss him out just like he cussed everyone else out.

That was my experience of a father: someone who couldn't be trusted, a man who lied, used and abused his family. He put on a front for a lot of people, but I knew him for what he really was. He had called me every type of bitch and whore in the book. He told me that I was unwanted and would never amount to anything, because I was dumb. Not once did he try to initiate a healthy father-daughter relationship. He never got to know me. If he saw me cry, he would just look past me and not ask what upset me. He was very passive, withdrawn, and unemotional towards me. No affection came from him. I was always aware of the tension in the air when he was around and was in constant defense mode. I didn't feel protected, and I definitely didn't call him dad.

Fathers are supposed to be protectors. They give you identity and guidance. Fathers are to be loving, responsive, active, and involved. They are to be loving even in discipline. They are to be an earthly example of God our Father. I did not have that and, even though I was told God was a good Father, I couldn't see Him that way. I had major father wounds. Having those wounds will distort your view of God. I didn't know what a good father looked like, and I couldn't imagine God that way. And honestly, it sounded weird to me!

I've since forgiven my father and, as I became an adult and gave my life to Christ, I began to see him differently. I learned how to show him grace and mercy. How to honor him. I knew he couldn't give me what he didn't have. He couldn't love me and treat me like a loving father should because he didn't know how. He didn't know Jesus and had no concept of what a good father looked like. I personally apologized to him when I realized my own wrongs and made things right. Although he was wrong for the things he did and said, I was wrong, too. I forgave him for how he treated me as well. I will be honest; this forgiveness took time. I had to continue to forgive and be mindful of my thoughts and feelings towards him and really dig up the bitterness I had.

As he observed how I now treated him as a new Christian, he began to believe. He watched my transformation, and I noticed how our relationship began to change. My son, at times, would minister to him too. He would watch me closely in my early walk with Christ and start to inquire about Jesus. He would ask me questions and I would even find him reading the bible and discussing topics with my mom.

God is incomparable, unchangeable, and loving far above any earthly father. Even if you know you have the best father on earth, God is ten million times better. The very character and nature of God is love. HE is a truth-speaking, infinite, holy, long-suffering GOD. He is sovereign and unequal. It took me a long time to grasp the revelation that He is indeed a good father. I would worship and pray, but in the back of my mind have a backup plan in case God failed me in case He didn't come through for me. God is trustworthy and there is no need for a backup plan with Him.

You see, I saw Him mostly as a Master and not a Father. I found it hard to be "intimate" with Him because I had a distorted view of intimacy. It was extremely difficult to receive His love. But I thank God that He initiates relationships and relentlessly pursues us. He is so patient and gentle with us, but not in a weak way. Not once did He pressure me and force me into a relationship with Him. He invited me and I answered.

Spending time with God in the beginning was awkward to me and I didn't understand it. I didn't think I was good enough to be able to just go before a perfect God. I tried everything in my power to think and do good things, then go to God. I was always tense when it came to the thought of spending time with God. Not realizing that there were unresolved father wounds from my adopted father, I was projecting my view of my natural father figures on God.

I finally came to the end of myself and sought God for healing. I cried and cried my little heart out before Him. I laid it all out and told Him everything. All my insecurities about trusting Him completely. I laid them before Him, telling Him of every hurt and emotional pain. It took me a few hours, but by the end of it, I felt so good.

And, literally, the next couple of months God showed up. I decided that I would trust Him and have faith in Him as a Father. And He has never ever let me down. The bible says that He is a very present help in trouble (Psalm 46:1). Whenever I had those feelings and thoughts of God not being there for me, I would catch myself and remind myself of who God is. And God did not disappoint. He answered my prayers, provided for me, and protected me. Most of my encounters with Him happened through my dreams. He would show up and answer my prayers with instructions and when I woke up, I'd have the interpretation.

Jesus is the one and only true living God, the only God that can speak, the only God that can deliver. There is no other God besides Him. His name is Jesus!

#BeautyForAshes

I saw a quote that said, "With God, suffering is not the final outcome." It tells me that with God there is hope! We may suffer many things on this earth but that's not the end. Far from it!

God is the master renovator! He replaces the dirty marks or ashes in our lives with beauty. He takes the shame, grief, and brokenness and redeems us, cleanses us, and makes us new. That is what God has done in my life. This is my testimony of who God is! You do not have to sit in your ashes! God can and will redeem you and make you even more beautiful than before. Its more than a cleaning work, it's a renovating work! I never imagined being free from depression and shame. And now I am doing more than just being free, I am helping others.

And can I be honest? IT took A LOT for me to get here. I am here as an example to those who would receive my message of hope. God sent so many people my way to help pick me up and put me back on my path. I've stumbled so often and wasted so much time. I am grateful that I am not where I used to be.

But time is of the essence. We don't have a lot of time here on earth to be playing around. I urge you to make your choice to receive salvation, accept Jesus as your lord and savior and serve God. You don't know when you will die: the devil is real; he knows his time is running out and he wants you to perish with him. He wants to deceive you and distract you from the truth.

Thank you so much for reading my story! I am so happy to be able to share my experience and tell you all about the saving power of God. His demonstration of love, power, and grace over my life is so amazing. I hope you see Him as a loving Father and a mighty Deliverer. Without Him I had no hope, no expectations, and no future. Because of Him I can boldly tell my story with no shame or condemnation. Jesus is the way, the truth, and the life. I hope you continue to follow along with me as I release more of my story. This is just the beginning!

Follow me on Facebook at Danielle Holder
On Instagram at its_danielle_holder
On YouTube at AdoptedPrincess
My website at danielleholder.com

Acknowledgements

I want to acknowledge a few people for their contributions and help with getting this project out and into the hands of those who need this story!

Amanda Larry, one of my best friends, and book cover designer! There were many times I put this project down and walked away, but you were there to encourage me to pick it back up.

Chaunte Mills, my inspiration and encourager. You were like my midwife in the spirit that helped me push this big-headed baby out! I could not have done this without your direction, prayers, and expertise.

Taneesha Dorn! My best friend and sister from another mister! Thank you for your patience, prayers, encouragement, and friendship! You have no idea how much you have impacted my life, and for that I am forever grateful. Thank you for our early morning prayers and bible studies! You are a real one!

Everyone who continued to ask and encourage me to get this story out and published, THANK YOU! There were so many people along the way who came and dropped knowledge, encouragement, and prayers. I am grateful for you all!

I also want to give a huge thank you to a few people that God sent my way to lift me up when I was on the verge of quitting. Bishop Alfred Fowler in Wilmington, Delaware: he was the first preacher to share the gospel with me. Pastor Carl Wright in Columbus, Ohio: he played a major role in my life! He stayed faithful to his assignment that God gave him for my life, and through prayer and preaching, helped save my life. Apostle Timothy Brinson in Philadelphia, PA: y'all not going find a more anointed prophet and preacher on the east coast! He literally prophesied me right back on track and pastored me until my move to Ohio. Janaya Jackson: one of the most anointed therapists! She was the first therapist I chose to see as an adult. I would not be able to author this book today if it had not been for her! Thank you! And lastly Apostle Brian Williams, my current pastor in Columbus, Ohio. I almost gave up, again! But he remained faithful to his call and literally preached me back on track when I threw in the towel after my parents passed.

Resources

The first and most important resource is the Bible. Please get a bible, a study bible if you can, that will help you understand the word. Join a local church that believes in the whole bible. Surround yourself with other bible-believing Christians. And, if needed, get counseling and professional help for your trauma.

List of recommended reads:
Touched: And it was our little secret by Carl D. Wright
Exposing the wicked to step into righteousness by C. Mills
Belonging by Janaya Jackson
Abba: Experience God as Father and Redeem your Failure, Hurt, and Pain by Dr. Matthew Stevenson
The Armor of God by Priscilla Shirer

Other Resources:

If you ever experience suicidal thoughts, GO to the emergency room: this is a medical emergency. If you are experiencing a mental health crisis, but not wanting to harm yourself or anyone else, here are some resources that may help:

National Suicide Prevention Lifeline: 1-800-273-8255

NAMI- national alliance on mental health: nami.org

Psychology Today: psychologytoday.com: this resource helps you find counselors near you that fit your preferences (gender, insurance, payment, area of expertise/specialty).

Openpathcollective.com: Affordable counseling database

www.ingramcontent.com/pod-product-compliance
Lightning Source LLC
Chambersburg PA
CBHW030913080526
44589CB00010B/282